Arcana In Seventeen Syllables

J L McPherson

BookLeaf Publishing

India | USA | UK

Made with ❤ on the BookLeaf Publishing Platform
www.bookleafpub.in
www.bookleafpub.com

Dedication

To Brooke and Ezra, my shining lights.

Preface

The Fool stands at the edge of the
unknown, gazing out over the
vast landscape before them. With
a heart full of curiosity and a
satchel of endless possibility,
they take a step forward—not in
certainty, but in trust. The
journey has begun.

Like The Fool, this collection of
haiku embraces the spirit of
exploration. Each poem is a
moment suspended in seventeen
syllables, a fleeting glimpse into

the mysteries of the Major Arcana. The Tarot has long been a mirror for the human experience—cycles of growth, loss, revelation, and renewal. In its twenty-one numbered cards, we find our own stories woven into symbols, archetypes, and lessons.

I began this project much like The Fool, not knowing exactly where it would lead. With each haiku, I sought to distill the essence of a card—not in rigid interpretation, but in feeling, in imagery, in the quiet space between words. Some poems came as sudden flashes of insight, others unfolded slowly, like a card drawn with careful intention.

To read Tarot is to trust intuition. To write haiku is to embrace brevity, to find depth in simplicity. Both require us to slow down, to observe, to listen to what is not immediately spoken.

So, dear reader, consider this book an invitation. Step lightly, with an open heart, and let the words lead you where they will. Like The Fool, take the first step—there is wisdom in the journey.

Acknowledgements

Special thanks to Greg Brockton, Tim Ferriss and Atticus O'Sullivan.

I. The Magician

Hands weave light and air,
a spell of becoming cast,
the world awakens.

II. The High Priestess

Moonlight on still waves,
secrets whisper in silence,
only she listens.

III. The Empress

Spring rain feeds the roots,
flowers bloom in quiet grace,
a mother's soft touch.

IV. The Emperor

Stone walls guard the land,
order forged from dust and will,
a throne stands firm.

V. The Hierophant

Ancient hands unfold,
rituals shape the seeking,
truth hides in symbols.

VI. The Lovers

Two paths intertwine,
hearts move like birds on warm
winds,
one choice, one journey.

VII. The Chariot

Wheels carve dust and sky,
fists clenched, eyes fixed on the
road,
the storm bows to me.

VIII. Strength

A hand tames the beast,
not by force, but by soft grace,
a breath, a whisper.

IX. The Hermit

Lantern's glow on stone,
footsteps echo into dark,
the stars wait above.

X. Wheel of Fortune

Gold leaves spin in air,
fortune shifts like restless tides,
all things rise and fall.

XI. Justice

A feather, a blade,
truth rests in quiet balance,
the scales do not lie.

XII. The Hanged Man

Upside-down he sees,
stillness is its own motion,
truth in surrender.

XIII. Death

Autumn leaves descend,
the branch shivers and exhales,
new buds dream in sleep.

XIV. Temperance

Water meets the flame,
one cools, the other rises
a bridge of balance.

XV. The Devil

Chains that feel like silk,
shadows grin behind bright eyes,
the door is open.

XVI. The Tower

Lightning splits the sky,
stone and pride fall together,
the storm begins new.

XVII. The Star

A hand lifts water,
stars sing where silence once
dwelled,
hope glows on the waves.

XVIII. The Moon

Fog curls over fields,
a lone wolf howls at the glow,
truth hides in dreamlight.

XIX. The Sun

Bare feet on warm grass,
laughter bursts like golden
beams,
morning kisses all.

XX. Judgement

Echoes rise from dust,
footsteps call back forgotten
names,
awake, step forward.

XXI. The World

The circle is whole,
one journey ends as one starts,
the wind knows my name.

www.ingramcontent.com/pod-product-compliance
Lightning Source LLC
LaVergne TN
LVHW021339200726
843509LV00014B/2581